Thoughts at Crossings

Charlotte Lit Press
Charlotte Center for Literary Arts, Inc.
PO Box 18607
Charlotte, NC 28218
charlottelit.org/press

Cover photo by Allison Batley on Unsplash

ISBN: 978-1-960558-05-3

PROUD MEMBER

[clmp]

COMMUNITY OF LITERARY MAGAZINES & PRESSES
W W W . C L M P . O R G

Thoughts at Crossings

Linda Vigen Phillips

CHARLOTTE**LIT**
P R E S S
Charlotte Center for Literary Arts, Inc.
Charlotte, North Carolina
charlottelit.org

In loving memory of Patricia Ann Skelton,
whole sister at last.

I don't want to end up simply having visited this world.

~Mary Oliver

I want to start with truth and end with art.

~Ocean Vuong

Contents

Sunday Afternoon Visits

Our mountain town touted more sun than clouds, giving
me a quirky sense of pride that home could be like that—
sunny all the time. Sunday afternoons in the 1960s, we went
for drives to soak it in. Or people dropped in to see us, usually

my sister Patty, her husband Jim, and their kids. I still lived
with our mother and my father—a bored teenager, soon to be
first in our family to college. In my mind, that fact set me apart
from their pointless small talk. Yet the talk pulled me. I longed

for those sounds of normalcy: Patty, with her flushed cheeks
accepting Mother's offer of leftover pie. Jim and my father
trading war stories over beers—their tales peppered with son-
of-bitch expletives. Mother chain smoking while swinging

that one leg back and forth. Still, I was relieved when my father
handed me the car keys, some cash to take the kids to the DQ.
My hunger for the ordinary as palpable as the curl on top
a smooth vanilla cone. It drove me. After Patty passed,

Jim called—fulfilling her deathbed wish—to tell me what Patty
had confessed on their wedding night: My father had stolen her
innocence. The sun shifted that day. All that light and I missed it.
The venom in her eyes at his vulgar stories. The way she never

spoke to him directly. That piece of apple pie she hid behind.
How she kept that secret, kept the sun shining all our lives.

Our Mother

was valedictorian
played piano
painted with oils
like a Rembrandt

rape muddied the palette
smudged the vision
canvas and brush
stopped singing

leaving my sister and me
brokenness no
one could fix and
a masterpiece

In the Ditch

Mother wakes me, panicked
middle of the night.
Get dressed. Your father needs you.
My heart races like the motor I hear outside.
Pulling on crumpled clothes,
it's his brand-new brown tweed suit
I picture, hair slicked with Brylcreem
ready for the annual Weyerhaeuser dinner.

*Get him out of that damned car
before he wakes the neighbors.*
He listens to you. They all listen to me.
Bartenders at the VFW, the American Legion,
Johnny's Corner. Weekend after weekend.
They know me by name.

I step out back for the short walk
to the ditch across the street, feet
crunch loud, waking neighbors
not already stationed behind closed curtains.

A muddied pantleg hangs out the driver's door,
his sprawled body behind the wheel
digging that ditch deep with his drunken right foot.
He gives up without a fight when I grasp
the wrinkled suit to drag him out
of the tilted car. Like an obedient child
he lets me stagger him to the door where she stands
silhouetted in the eerie glow,
every light on in the house.

From What I Can Gather

What I know about her is scattered like prairie dust
swirling across sagebrush and juniper
in the Oregon high desert where she grew up.
Sheepherders and cattlemen tracked the barnyard
into her father's hotel, into my grandmother's
fine dining room, into the parlor where my mother
beguiled them not with beauty—that belonged
to her mother—but brilliance. Hard-drinking
ranchers unschooled in Chopin, Beethoven,
mesmerized by this desert flower in full bloom,
dropping "Moonlight Sonata" petal by petal.

Maybe a cattle-driving rancher gave into the Siren
call drifting through the transom. Or a traveling
salesman overtaken by this melodious wildflower.
Down a dim-lit hall one night after her final piece,
my mother was violated. My grandfather shoved
the piano into a corner and sent her away.

This part I know from hospital records.
My grandmother gave her money for nursing school.
She was found penniless and naked on the streets
of Portland after vagrants tried to assault her.
It was a test from God, she said from city jail
where she claimed to perform miracles,
see visions of the cross and angels. She spent
three months hospitalized, then returned
to the hotel. The piano was gone.

Helping Mommy Pack for Our Trip

The dark kitchen held no dinner.
Her voice was far but near,
this game unfamiliar.
Daddy should be home soon.

Get your dolly...your bristly distly brushly lushly
ukulele playlee...

    Mommy, you're funny.

There now, my rosary...yes...my rosy rosary missal...see
be a good girlie...my nightgown...

    We really going away, Mommy?

and talcum powder, see...talcum...palcum

    talcum palcum...talcum palcum
    Daddy's shaving cream?

I watched her sprinkle talcum snowballs
all over her brown dress.
The door whooshed open.
The sound of Daddy's lunch pail
slamming down, the way he
shouted her name,
how twilight shadows
bounced around the room.

The next morning
he took her to the hospital
and left me home.
Grandma came
to clean up the mess.

Cracks Have a Reason

The dark morning tried to swallow me whole.
I searched out the window for anything breathing,
a mama bear and her cubs, maybe a doe and her fawns.

We left before dawn, my father and I, for the drive
to the Oregon State Mental Hospital, four hours to imagine
trying to talk to my sick mother.

By the time we returned,
the sky might be splashed with a blood red sunset,
the same color my panties were that day I got my period

and my mannequin-mom cracked into pieces. *The supplies
are in the hall closet,* she had said through a cloud of smoke,
one leg pumping the air around the porch chair.

She didn't need to put out her cigarette or come inside
to show me where the supplies were. I knew she had
stuffed them behind the towels on the top shelf.

I didn't need her to show me how to thread the pad
through those metal claws dangling from the stretchy belt.
Health class took care of that.

I needed her soft, warm hand reaching out to me—
tender belly, trembling shoulders, tear-stained cheeks—
tell me, mother, how it was with you on your day.
Will you?

How Mental Illness Has Its Way

It followed my mother in the door after
every hospital visit, that
psych ward scent, trailing
stale blue smoke. Tracked
in mud would clean up better but
nothing calmed nerves like
her Marlboros. The stench drenched
downy pillows, settled to the bone
at night, dirtied
morning air.

I worried into dark
insomnia, will I come down with
this malady like a common cold
or will crazy genes lie dormant
waiting for the right sunny day
to strike?

How soon before I pace and drift, window
to window? *That car down
the road is watching us up here on
the hill.* When will
I clang and babble, insist
we are under siege?

What If I go catatonic and they
whisk me off to shock treatments?

I might blush in shame. Tell the doctor
it's my mother's plague.
Or maybe I will say, "No, no this can't be
real. Not me. I'm not the crazy
in our family."

Swimming Lessons

My mother smiled from the bleachers as I shivered, dripped
my way to the class where I was already late. I didn't jump in

like the shrill voice commanded. They watched me slide down,
my head safe above water. A kind girl greeted me by name.

I wiped my dry face with a wet hand to cover the tears. I could
pass Beginners today by doing the front crawl over and back

at the deep end, breathe and blow, breathe and blow, breathe
and…all week there wasn't a right time to tell the shrill voice

I breathe in bigger than I breathe out. Three gulps and my lungs
implode. I could drown in the deep end, didn't she know?

After a lifetime of waters lapping at my feet, oceans daring
me beyond breakers, I know my fear didn't begin in the deep

end. It began in the waves of my mother's womb, flotsam
from that night of terror in her father's hotel, naked shame

in a Portland jail, shock treatment jolts, long psyche ward stays.
All this she carried into my beginning; I breathed it in.

I cannot fault her. She knew rough waters. She knew before
I did, I would need to learn to swim.

Thoughts at Crossings

I walked across the Eleventh Street Bridge almost every day
on my way to and from Crawford Hills High or town

or anywhere. Under cover of singing gulls, swooping pelicans,
I whispered truth my best friends didn't know—

that I had a mother with bipolar disorder who was sleeping
off the effects of her medicine when I got home. That she

wasn't really visiting relatives all those times I stayed
at Aunt Nellie's. That one time, right before they took her

back to the hospital for more shock treatments,
the police brought her home in a paddy wagon.

They'd found her half-naked, clinging to the sign:
Bridge Ices Before Road. At every crossing, I couldn't stop

thinking jealous thoughts about my friends' moms
who sewed prom dresses, ran the PTA, didn't freak out

over their daughters' first periods. Mothers who remember
friends' names, smile through endless boy-talk.

At every crossing, the thought of jumping
pulled me like a magnet toward the railing.

All that stopped me was the image of slime green
canal water closing over my head.

Movie Night

I drip slushy snow into the popcorn warmth
of the Esquire Theater lobby,
a five-year old's delight at being out after dark
anything you want from the concession stand, baby—
before the three of us take our seats in the crowded theater.

The auditorium darkens, the big screen screams out
loud music, razzle-dazzle lights, a parade of ladies dressed
unlike my mother, in items I would not know to name—
a Burlesque wardrobe of tasseled pasties,
rhinestone bras, crystal fringed corsets, feather boas and fans.

His wheedling pleas
to take care of his needs,
cajoling my mother
to go along with it and bring me:
she's too young to remember, over her head,
it will be alright, honey, and hey, it will be good for us,
if you know what I mean.

The whole picture is no longer over my head.
I know now how the theme from that movie
played out in our back-porch bedroom that same year.
He stripped my sister raw in the dead of night.
It will never be alright.

How it Was Sharing that Back Porch Bed

The bedroom we shared was a back porch
      forced into being something it wasn't—
         a space where two sisters slept
a cast iron bed shoved tight
      against the wall so a skinny
five-year-old didn't fall out,
      protected by the stronger one
on the outside edge.

A shepherd was tasked
with lying across the opening to the sheepfold
so the wolf must breach his body
to penetrate the flock.

You also had other duties. You had to pass
      dishwashing inspection, housekeeping inspection,
schoolwork inspection, body inspection—
      his eyes.

On the nights when the wolf crept in, you must have done
      what you needed to do
         so that I, the lamb, slept on.

The Night My Sister Started Dying

Even at four, I knew my father knew
many wondrous things about trees.
My teen half-sister knew it too
but she leaned away from him
like an oak resisting gale wind.

Trees afflicted with sooty bark disease are stuck
dying, my father said. A passerby doesn't detect
when roots are ravaged with decay. The leaves
still make shade at the hot end of summer,
he said. The stuck part of death doesn't show
until it's too late to save it.

After my father crowded the bed
she and I shared, next to me, my sister
lay naked, passed out in her own vomit and blood.
I have no recollection nor did she ever
divulge the damage he did
by forced entry to the taproot of her soul.

After She Died, I Learned She Stopped Him with a Knife

Their screaming woke me. I hovered
in the kitchen
corner, watching
my father rage,

my mother plead, my sister wield
something. That's it.
The memory
fades there, flitting
bird-like in my head all my life.

How Does Your Garden Grow?

I recall your lush garden
petunias thrived
under your thumb
speaking volumes

about your ability to
cultivate seeds
nurture new life
create beauty

out of the soil, into the soul.
Father, what turned your trowel
so foul?
Damned petunias.

Cost Analysis

It's a headshot of my father.
It held her gaze as she
penciled oaths and longings
to him during the war.
Now decayed scotch tape
curls, cracks, fails
to repair
the rip—
a jagged bolt
of lightening across
both cheeks
and the bridge of his nose.

I wonder what came
at a higher price—
horizontally slashing
the nose bone in half
or later, pulling fresh tape
from a dispenser
to repair the damage.

Forgiveness

I tried this on today
to see how it fit and I remembered
how the twinkle in my father's eyes dimmed
that morning we went fishing on Wood River,
his tongue loosened without alcohol.
There was nothing left for him, he said
when his mother died too early.
He hopped a box car and headed west,
a teenager about my age
packing a soul full of holes.

The early dawn butter-sun
warmed the meadow grass
into sweet anticipation of rainbow trout.
We watched for our lines to tug.
I swear I could see his heart
struggle like a rusty lure on a snag
just under the clear rippling water.

What We Sisters Have to Bear

What did you think that day
when I called to say *I'm coming
home to be married, can you
throw a reception together?*
Was the familiarity—so easy for me—
something for you to bear?

Did you relive the dusty
drive to Reno, your hasty elopement,
your only reception the desk clerk
at Motel-6 signing you and Jim in
for your one-night honeymoon?

Did long-smoldering smut flare up,
re-ignite when you remembered—again
your escape from our house
trailing the rancid stench
of my father's abuse?

Small pittance for me now
to bear the weight of that phone call
and all the times you rescued me,
while you never once let me see
the debris field he made of you.

For Survivors to Consider

Survivors walk away from the scene,
blood-splattered, bruised not broken,
limping not lame,
defined forever by their life

after—unlike victims,
trapped by shrapnel embedded
beneath a superficial scar
masking the potential
for the trauma to turn toxic.

Forgive me. I never understood
how my walking away
reminded you
that you could not.

Valley of Baca

Sister, we might have made a pilgrimage together, the journey out of that barren bedroom where we crowded on top of a coiled mattress, squeaking like a desert llama at every turn. We might have made our way together towards the Holy City of reconciling, early on, if you had not set out so abruptly in that peach organdy dress Grandma gave you, with the Peter Pan collar and flared skirt with velveteen swirls. How I longed to rub my hands across that soft material one more time before you left.

In my sticky-finger childhood I never guessed that you saw in me the same oval chin, the same Nordic eyes as my father, the man who stole your innocence like a marauder in the wilderness. I never guessed that the bulwark in my life was the same rapist of your body and soul. No wonder your feet could not carry you fast enough away from me, into your own caravan of early marriage, children, the suburban house, all the succulence the desert could not sustain.

We traveled the highways to Zion by separate passage all our lives. How I longed for you to grab my little-sister hand through the craggy gulches of mental illness that ravaged our mother, yet I knew you were there, out there in the same dust storm as me, moving through the boulder-like breakdowns to the bumpy scree of one day at a time.

The night he died. You mothered our mother. You put me up in the master bedroom without a single consoling word. You did not look me in the eye. I was still in the dark when I went to bed, stifling sobs beneath a pillow.

I came to you when it was clear your journey was ending. You had reached the crest where the first glimpse of weeping balsams appeared down the valley like a wavy desert mirage. I hoped you could smell the lush green perfume as my tears anointed our clasped hands. I felt the release as you kicked off your sandals and raced toward the wellspring in the soft, warm sand.

Acknowledgements

Thanks to North Carolina Poetry Society's Poetry in Plain Sight for publishing "Cost Analysis."

Heartfelt thanks to Kathie Collins and Paul Reali, founders of Charlotte Center for Literary Arts, fondly known by the writing community as Charlotte Lit. I appreciate all the workshops, readings, and special programs they offer, especially the Chapbook Lab from which this chapbook was born. Special thanks to Dannye Romine Powell who so expertly taught, nurtured, and supported us through the year of workshops and to my mentor, Jessica Jacobs, who patiently challenged me to new levels of craft and creativity through keen critiquing and sharing of wisdom.

I would be remiss without a special thanks to each member of the Chapbook Lab who became the best and least expensive therapy group in town: Vivian Bikulege, John Clark, Kathie Collins, Patricia Joslin, Brooke Lehmann, Gary Phillips, Betty Ritz Rogers, Eric Sbarge, Joe Spencer, and Lucinda Trew. And to my longest-standing writing buddy, Carol Baldwin: thank you for being the first reader of almost everything I write, and then often going the extra mile.

Finally, to my husband, Wendell: I have been blessed by your encouragement and support over the years, not to mention the grammar mistakes you always seem to find!

About the Author

Linda Vigen Phillips is the author of two young adult novels in verse, *Crazy* (Eerdmans Books, 2014, re-released 2024) and *Behind These Hands* (Light Messages, 2018), an Eric Hoffer Award winner, as well as numerous poems in literary magazines. An active mental health advocate, she is co-founder of Charlotte Clubhouse, a unique and proven international model serving persons with mental illnesses. Linda grew up in rural Oregon, and has lived the past 33 years in Charlotte, North Carolina, with her husband Wendell.

Printed in the USA
CPSIA information can be obtained
at www.ICGtesting.com
JSHW081106241023
50721JS00005B/114